WHICH CAME FIRST?

COMMUNICATION INVENTIONS

FROM HIEROGLYPHICS TO DVDs

by Jacqueline A. Ball and Gabriel Kaufman

Consultant: Paul F. Johnston, Washington, D.C.

BEARPORT
PUBLISHING COMPANY, INC.

New York, New York

Credits:
Cover and title page, Michelle Barera (illustrator), clipart.com (telephone and radio); 4, Comstock Production Department/Alamy; 5(T), Corbis; 5(B), Michael Dunning/Getty; 6, Kenneth Garrett/ National Geographic Image Collection; 7(T) Pete Leonard/Corbis; 7(B) Douglas Pulsipher/Alamy; 8, Mitch Hrdlicka/ Getty; 9(T), PhotoAlto/Superstock; 9(B) age footstock/Superstock; 10, Getty/ Archive Holdings Inc; 11(T), Leonard de Selva/Corbis; 11(B), Bettman/Corbis; 12, Kim Karpeles/ Alamy; 13(T), Stockdisc/Getty; 13(B), AP Photo/Eric Gay; 14, AP Photo; 15(T), Powerstock/ Superstock; 15(B), Jacob August Riis/Corbis; 16, Gernsheim Collection, Harry Ransom Humanities Research Center, The University of Texas at Austin; 17(T), Rex Argent/Alamy; 17(B), Bettmann/ Corbis; 18, Corbis; 19(B), AP Photo/Massimo Sambucetti/POOL AP; 20, Jules Frazier/Getty; 21(T), Stockdisc/Getty; 21(B), AP Photo; 22, Laurence Dutton/Getty; 23(T), Photodisc Blue/ Getty; 23(B), AP Photo/Christopher MorrisVII; 24, AP Photo/Eric Rosenberg; 25(T), Science and Society Photo Library; 25(B), AP Photo/Koji Sasahara;

Design and production by Dawn Beard Creative and Octavo Design and Production, Inc.

Library of Congress Cataloging-in-Publication Data

Ball, Jacqueline A.
  Communication inventions : from hieroglyphics to DVDs / by Jacqueline A. Ball and Gabriel Kaufman.
    p. cm. — (Which came first?)
  Includes bibliographical references and index.
  ISBN 1-59716-129-2 (library binding) — ISBN 1-59716-136-5 (pbk.)
  1. Telecommunication—Juvenile literature. 2. Mass media—Juvenile literature.
I. Kaufman, Gabriel. II. Title. III. Series.

TK5102.4.B36 2006
621.382—dc22
                    2005029885

For more information, write to Bearport Publishing Company, Inc., 101 Fifth Avenue, Suite 6R, New York, New York 10003. Printed in the United States of America.

1 2 3 4 5 6 7 8 9 10

Contents

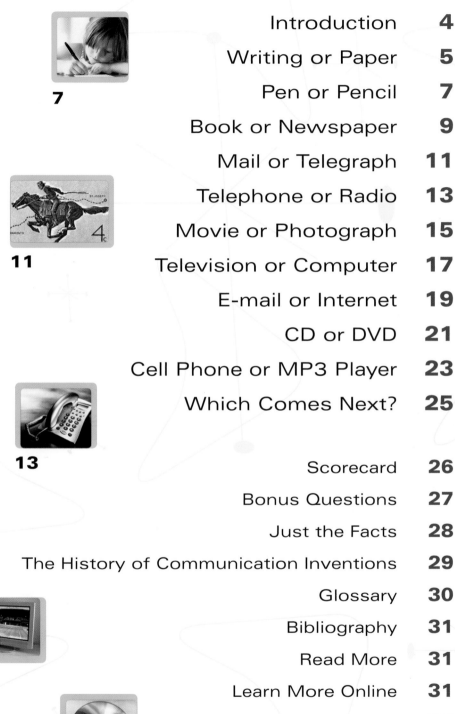

Introduction

You're watching TV when you hear exciting news. A movie star is coming to your town! You rush to the phone to call your friends, then change your mind. You'll send an e-mail instead. Now you can tell everyone at once.

Television, movies, telephones, and e-mail are all ways to **communicate** with other people. This book describes ten pairs of communication inventions. Read about each pair and guess which one came first. Then turn the page for the answer.

Turn the page to find out which came first.

Which Came First?

Writing

Before writing was invented, people could only communicate by speaking. Sometimes they mixed up things, or forgot important details. It could make everyday life very confusing!

▲ When stories are told out loud, they can change depending on who tells them. When stories are written down, they stay the same forever.

Paper

Try making a shopping list without using paper. It's hard to find something other than paper that you can write on easily and tuck in your pocket.

◀ We use paper so much that we barely notice it, but paper would be very hard to live without.

Answer: Writing

Some of the first writing was really drawing. In about 3000 B.C., the Egyptians carved pictures called **hieroglyphics** into stone. These pictures became an alphabet.

The Chinese invented paper more than 2,000 years later. In the meantime, people wrote on **papyrus**, animal skins, and even bones. Imagine putting *those* in your pocket!

◀ **Hieroglyphics inside a tomb**

In Thailand, you can buy paper made from elephant dung. One elephant provides enough dung for 115 sheets of paper per day.

Which Came First?

Turn the page to find out which came first.

Don't worry—there's no squid juice in your pen. The ink in most pens today is made of dye and water.

Pen

Pens make their mark with ink. Some ink comes from an unlikely source: squid. To scare off enemies, squid spray black **fluid** into the water. That fluid is used to make **sepia** ink.

Pencil

The "lead" in pencils isn't really lead. It's graphite, a soft **mineral** found underground. (This is a good thing, since lead is poisonous.)

If you took a pencil and drew a line until the lead ran out, the line would be about 35 miles (56 km) long!

7

Answer: Pen

In about 2000 B.C., the Egyptians turned hollow reeds into pens. A thousand years later, **quill pens** became popular.

Pencils came along in 1564, when a huge graphite mine was discovered in England. Erasers weren't attached to pencils until 1858. Before erasers, people used bread crumbs to rub out mistakes.

◀ **The Declaration of Independence and the U.S. Constitution were both written with quill pens.**

Pencils can even write underwater!

Turn the page to
find out which
came first.

Which Came First?

Book

Books used to be copied by hand. Imagine writing down the whole dictionary! These days, **printing presses** make books at super-high speeds.

◄ This printing press moves quickly. In 2001, one company printed two Harry Potter books *per second*!

Newspaper

Fifty-six million newspapers are sold daily in the United States. That's a lot of news! Some papers include crossword puzzles, **horoscopes**, and comic strips, too.

◄ Newspapers from around the world are also sold in the United States.

Answer: Newspaper

The first newspaper, *Acta Diurna* (*Daily Events*), was published in Rome in 131 B.C. The paper wasn't delivered to people's homes. Instead, it was posted on stone, metal, or wooden tablets around town so citizens could read the news.

Diamond Sutra is the oldest printed book ever found with a date inside: A.D. 868. Carved wooden blocks were dipped in ink and pressed on paper to make the book.

What do Walt Disney, Martin Luther King, Jr., and Wayne Gretzky have in common? They all worked as newspaper delivery boys when they were young.

Turn the page to
find out which
came first.

Which Came First?

▲ Most Pony Express riders were teenagers.
The youngest was just 11 years old.

Mail

For 39 cents, you can send a letter anywhere in the United States. During the days of the Pony Express, a letter cost about five dollars to send!

Telegraph

Urgent messages used to be sent by telegraph. An operator tapped out letters in **Morse code**. The taps traveled over a wire. Then another operator turned the taps back into words.

▲ The telegraph used to be an important means of
communication. Today the telegraph isn't used
much. However, many ships, including U.S.
space shuttles, still keep a telegraph key on
board in case of an emergency.

Answer: Mail

China had mail as early as 4,000 years ago. In the United States, the post office was **established** in 1775. U.S. mail has been carried by steamboat, stagecoach, mule, horse, and even sled dog.

The first U.S. telegraph line was completed in 1844. In 1866, a telegraph wire connected America to Europe. It ran along the bottom of the Atlantic Ocean!

◄ **Most mail is carried by trucks and planes now, but there's still one mule route left in Supai, Arizona. Mules haul the mail to an Indian reservation below the rim of the Grand Canyon.**

A quick way to ask for help by telegraph is to tap out the letters "SOS." These letters were chosen because the Morse code for "SOS" is easy to remember.

Which Came First?

Telephone

You're on the phone when your call-waiting beeps. It's the dentist's office calling to remind you that you need a cleaning! You decide to ignore the call. Phones make it easy to communicate—or *not* to communicate!

▲ **If you have an emergency, you can dial 911 to get help. The 911 number was started in 1968.**

▲ **A flood victim listens to her radio in New Orleans after Hurricane Katrina.**

Radio

Can a radio save your life? When the electricity goes out, battery-powered radios are often the only source of information about storms and other **disasters**.

13

Answer: Telephone

Alexander Graham Bell invented the telephone in 1876, with help from Thomas Watson. The first words he said over the phone were, "Mr. Watson, come here. I want you!"

It's not as easy to name the inventor of the radio. Some people claim it was Guglielmo Marconi from Italy. Others say it was Nikola Tesla. Either way, the radio was born around 1900.

◀ **Bell's first telephone looked very different from today's telephones.**

The telephone was just one of Bell's inventions. In 1881, when President Garfield was shot, Bell quickly invented the metal detector in the hope of finding the bullet in Garfield's body.

Turn the page to
find out which
came first.

Which Came First?

Movie

Americans love going to the movies. More than 1.5 *billion* movie tickets were sold in 2004.

▲ **The average American eats about 59 quarts (65 l) of popcorn each year . . . most of it at the movies!**

▲ **A Riis photograph**

Photograph

Photos let people remember moments in their lives. They also communicate strong ideas. Jacob Riis took photographs of poor American families in the 1800s. His photos helped get new laws passed to help the poor.

15

Answer: Photograph

A Frenchman named Joseph Nicéphore Niépce took the first known photo in 1826. He called it a "heliograph," after the Greek words for "sun drawing."

In 1895, two other Frenchmen, brothers Louis and Auguste Lumière, showed the first movies to a paying audience.

▲ **The first known photograph is a picture of the view outside Niépce's window. Photography has come a long way since 1826!**

One of the Lumière brothers' movies was about a train. Legend has it that people were so afraid of the train rushing at them on the screen that they jumped out of their seats.

Turn the page to
find out which
came first.

Which Came First?

Television

How many channels can you watch on your television? When TV was invented, people were lucky to get *one* channel. Now, some viewers can get more than 500 channels.

▲ **Early TV shows were shown in black-and-white. Color TV didn't become popular until the 1960s.**

Computer

People take their computers everywhere—airplanes, coffee shops, and parks. Traveling would have been impossible with the first electronic computer. Why? It weighed *30 tons* (27 metric tons)!

▲ **The first electronic computer wasn't just heavy, it was also huge. It measured 1,800 square feet (167 square meters).**

17

Answer: Television

Philo T. Farnsworth, a scientist, helped **pioneer** television in the 1920s. The first program to draw a huge audience was the 1947 World Series. Many people bought their first TV sets just so they could watch the baseball games.

In 1946, American engineers introduced the first electronic computer. It cost $500,000 and took about 18 months to build.

◄ **Farnsworth and the first TV**

Ninety-eight out of 100 Americans have a TV in their house. The average American watches four hours of television per day.

Turn the page to
find out which
came first.

Which Came First?

E-mail
(Electronic Mail)

Sending letters and messages to people is not new. Sending them instantly to people around the globe is new. E-mail has changed the speed of communication forever.

Internet

Do you need to know why penguins can't fly or how to cook fried cactus? Try the Internet, where you can find information about almost anything. Remember to always check with your parents before using the Internet.

◄ **Even Pope John Paul II used the Internet.**

Answer: Internet

The Internet started in 1969 as a tool for the **military**. In 1989, Tim Berners-Lee created the World Wide Web (WWW), which made it easy for everyone to use the Internet.

Ray Tomlinson invented e-mail in 1971. He thought his invention was no big deal. He didn't dream that by 2005 more than 250 million people would use it daily.

▲ **People can go to Internet cafés to eat, socialize, and use the Internet all at the same time.**

"E-mail" is the nickname for electronic mail. What's snail mail? It's what some people call paper mail, which takes days rather than seconds to reach its destination.

Turn the page to
find out which
came first.

Which Came First?

CD (Compact Disc)

If you tell your grandmother you're burning a CD, she might grab the fire extinguisher! Just explain to her that "burning" means you're "recording." Then promise you'll never scare her like that again.

DVD (Digital Versatile Disc)

Not so long ago, you could see a movie only in a theater. Now you can rent one on DVD and watch it wherever and whenever you want.

◁ The best part about watching a DVD in the car is that you don't have to worry about someone tall sitting in front of you!

Answer: CD

James Russell thought up compact discs in 1965. However, companies didn't start selling them until the early 1980s. First came **audio** CDs for recording and playing music. Next, **CD-ROMs** were invented for storing computer files.

DVDs first went on sale in the mid-1990s. They can be used for the same purposes as CDs. They can also be used to record and play movies.

◀ **CDs last longer than records and sound much better than tapes and cassettes.**

At least ten different companies worked together to invent the DVD.

Which Came First?

Turn the page to find out which came first.

Cell (Cellular) Phone

Walk down the street almost anywhere and you'll see people talking to themselves. At least that's what it *looks* like they're doing, until you spot their tiny cell phones!

◄ **More than a billion people worldwide use cell phones.**

MP3 Player (also known as a Digital Audio Player)

Walk down that same street and chances are you'll see people singing to themselves, too! MP3 players let people carry **downloaded** music with them everywhere they go.

▲ **Even the president uses an MP3 player.**

23

Answer: Cell Phone

Dr. Martin Cooper invented the cell phone in 1973, but it took 20 years to catch on. Even then, people were amazed that they could talk on the phone outside their homes.

When MP3 players first appeared in the late 1990s, they weren't very popular. Then Apple Computer created the iPod in 2001. More than ten million iPods have been sold since then!

While Dr. Cooper was trying to invent the cell phone, a scientist at another company was rushing to do the same. Dr. Cooper's first cell-phone call was to his **rival**, telling him he had invented the phone first.

◀ **Dr. Cooper with the first cell phone. It was the size of a brick, and weighed nearly two pounds (1 kg).**

Which Comes Next?

Here are two new communication inventions that inventors are working on now. Which one do you think will catch on first?

Phone Tooth

The next time you go to the dentist for a filling, how about getting a phone instead? Sound from this tiny telephone travels up your jaw to your ear. One question: What happens when you brush?

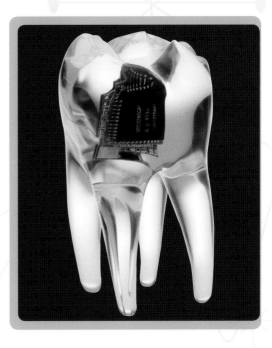

Bow-Lingual Translator

Who says communication is just for people? An electronic device around your dog's neck translates woofs and whines into words.

25

Scorecard

How many did you get correct?

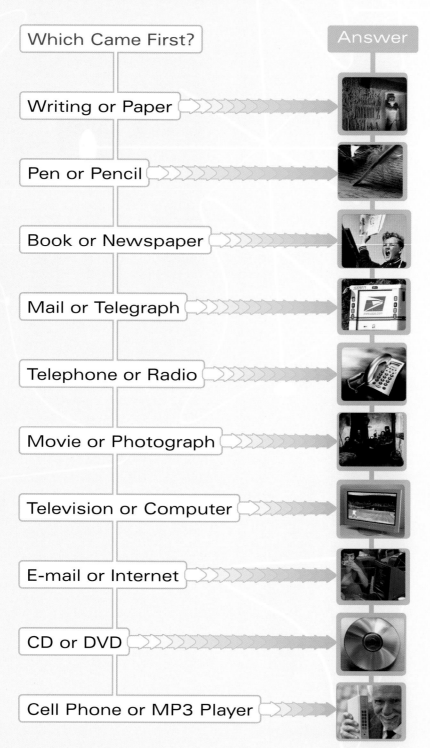

Which Came First?	Answer
Writing or Paper	
Pen or Pencil	
Book or Newspaper	
Mail or Telegraph	
Telephone or Radio	
Movie or Photograph	
Television or Computer	
E-mail or Internet	
CD or DVD	
Cell Phone or MP3 Player	

Bonus Questions

Now you know which of the communication inventions in this book came first. Here are a few bonus questions.

1. **How many inventions was Thomas Edison given credit for in his lifetime?**

    a. 1   b. 13   c. 197   d. 1,368

2. **Which of the following ways were used to deliver mail in the United States?**

    a. horse   c. dogsled

    b. mule   d. all of the above

3. **The youngest Pony Express rider was how old?**

    a. 15   b. 9   c. 18   d. 11

4. **We use an alphabet called the Roman alphabet. How many letters are in this alphabet?**

    a. 21   b. 23   c. 26   d. 28

5. **Television once showed only black-and-white pictures. When was the first color TV sold?**

    a. 1954   b. 1964   c. 1974   d. 1984

Just the Facts

* Philo T. Farnsworth was one of the biggest contributors to the creation of television. Farnsworth was born in a log cabin and rode a horse to school when he was a kid. He thought of the key idea for his invention while farming a potato field.

* The word telegraphy comes from two Greek words that together mean "writing over distance."

* The first radio transmission would have taken place in 1895 if a fire hadn't destroyed inventor Nikola Tesla's lab.

* American Sign Language (ASL) lets hearing-impaired people communicate with hand signals instead of sounds. It is the fourth most widely spoken language in the United States. Other countries have their own versions of sign language. Today's communication devices often have special features for the hearing-impaired.

The History of Communication Inventions

About 3000 B.C. Hieroglyphics developed

About 2000 B.C. First pens were used

131 B.C. *Acta Diurna*, the first newspaper

About A.D. 105 Paper invented in China

868 First printed book with date inside

1564 Pencil invented

1775 First post office in the United States

1826 First photograph taken

1844 First telegraph line in the United States

1876 Telephone invented

1895 First movies shown

About 1900 First radio

1920s First TV

1946 First electronic computer

1965 First CD

1969 First Internet is set up

1971 First e-mail sent

1973 First cell phone

Mid 1990s First DVDs

Late 1990s First MP3 player

Glossary

audio (AW-dee-oh)   having to do with how a sound is made or heard

CD-ROMs (SEE-DEE-ROMZ)   compact discs that can be read by a computer

communicate (kuh-MYOO-nuh-kate)   to share news, stories, and ideas with other people

disasters (duh-ZASS-turz)   events such as floods that cause great damage, loss, or suffering

downloaded (DOUN-*lohd*-ed)   transferred information from computer to a disk

established (ess-TAB-lished)   set up

fluid (FLOO-id)   liquid

hieroglyphics (*hye*-ur-uh-GLIF-iks)   writing used by ancient Egyptians, made up of pictures and symbols

horoscopes (HOR-uh-*skopes*)   diagrams of the positions of stars and planets based on people's birth dates; used to explain people's personalities and to predict events in their lives

military (MIL-uh-*ter*-ee)   having to do with soldiers and the armed forces

mineral (MIN-ur-uhl)   a substance found in nature; not a plant or an animal

Morse code (MORSS KODE)   a system that uses light or sound in a pattern of dots and dashes to represent letters

papyrus (puh-PYE-ruhss)   a tall plant that grows in water in northern Africa and southern Europe

pioneer (*pye*-uh-NIHR)   the first person to work in an unknown area

printing presses (PRINT-ing PRESS-uhz)   big machines that print books by pressing sheets of paper against a surface that has ink on it

quill pens (KWIL PENZ)   bird feathers dipped in ink

rival (RYE-vuhl)   a person that you are competing against

sepia (SEE-pee-uh)   an ink that is brownish in color

Bibliography

Casey, Susan. *Kids Inventing: A Handbook for Young Inventors.* Hoboken, NJ: John Wiley & Sons (2005).

Knauer, Kelly, ed. *Great Inventions: Geniuses and Gizmos: Innovations in Our Time.* New York: Time Inc. (2003).

Platt, Richard. *Communication: From Hieroglyphs to Hyperlinks.* Boston, MA: Houghton Mifflin (2004).

Wood, Richard, consulting editor. *Great Inventions.* Alexandria, VA: Time-Life Books (1995).

Read More

Ball, Jacqueline. *Getting the News.* New York: Sundance/Newbridge Educational Publishing (2005).

Oxlade, Chris. *Electronic Communication (Hello Out There).* London: Franklin Watts (1998).

Platt, Richard. *Technology and Communication.* Silver Dolphin (2001).

Learn More Online

Visit these Web sites to learn more about communication inventions:

http://inventors.about.com/library/inventors/bl_history_of_communication.htm

http://library.thinkquest.org/CR0211582

www.kidzworld.com/site/p5653.htm

Index

About the Authors

Jacqueline A. Ball has written and produced more than 100 books for kids and adults. She lives in New York City.

Although Gabriel Kaufman has never invented anything, he enjoys reading about other people who have. He works in children's publishing and lives in Brooklyn, New York.